Simple Delights

HERBS & SPICES

Simple Delights

HERBS & SPICES

a Salamander book

Salamander Books Limited
LONDON

A SALAMANDER BOOK

Published by Salamander Books Limited
129-137 York Way
London N7 9LG
United Kingdom

1 3 5 7 9 8 6 4 2

ISBN 0 86101 868 0

CREDITS

MANAGING EDITOR: Anne McDowall
DESIGNER: Carole Perks
RECIPES BY: Jo Craig, Linda Fraser, Kerenza Harries, Lesley Mackley,
Cecila Norman, Lorna Rhodes, Mary Trewby, Hilaire Walden.
PHOTOGRAPHERS: David Gill, Paul Grater, David Johnson, Sue Jorgensen,
Jon Stewart, Alister Thorpe.
FILMSET BY: SX Composing DTP
COLOUR REPRODUCTION: P & W Graphics Pte Ltd, Singapore
Printed and bound in Slovenia

CONTENTS

INTRODUCTION

The choice of herbs and spices is determined by the place as well as the particular food. We associate chervil, tarragon and marjoram with France; cumin and other curry spices with India; allspice with the West Indies; fresh ginger with Asia. And, of course, some spices and herbs are essential to a dish: no self-respecting Italian or Spanish cook would dream of making a risotto or paella without saffron, for instance. Here, as elsewhere, tradition plays an important role in the kitchen.

The traditions are based on centuries of wise experience, and on what is fashionable. This is particularly true when it comes to herbs. Until relatively recently, spices were expensive, highly prized commodities and in some cases worth more than their weight in gold. Products with such economic importance rarely are allowed to disappear from the market place. But herbs have never cost much, and the dividing line between a 'weed' and a herbs is a fine one. Dandelion, lovage and salad burnet, for example, were much used up until the end of the last century, then their culinary importance was all but forgotten, which is a pity, as many of the more unusual herbs such as these are excellent included in salads.

Herbs are often added as a garnish. Flowers used to be, and once more it's time to strew them in your salads and on desserts. Good food should taste wonderful and look beautiful.

PUMPKIN SOUP

1.5kg (3lb) pumpkin

25g (1oz/6 teaspoons) butter

1 onion, chopped

625ml (20fl oz/2½ cups)
chicken stock

1 teaspoon light brown sugar

good pinch grated nutmeg

¼ teaspoon paprika

salt and pepper

150ml (5fl oz/⅔ cup) single
(light) cream

3 slices bread

vegetable oil for frying

paprika

Discard pumpkin seeds and stringy bits. Cut out pumpkin flesh and dice. Melt butter in a large saucepan, add onion and cook until soft. Add pumpkin, stock and sugar, bring to the boil, then cover and simmer for 30 minutes. Purée, then return to pan. Stir in nutmeg, paprika, salt and pepper and cream. Reheat gently while making the garnish.

Stamp out either attractive shapes from bread or make rings using 2 cutters, 1 slightly larger than the other. Heat enough oil to come to a depth of 0.5cm (¼in) in a frying pan and cook bread until golden. Drain, then dust with paprika.

Serves 6.

CHILLED FISH SOUP

500g (1lb) unpeeled cooked prawns

2 strips lemon peel

2 bay leaves

2 blades mace

salt and pepper

4 small squid, cleaned and gutted

2 spring onions, green parts only, chopped

4 tomatoes, skinned, seeded and chopped

2 tablespoons peeled and chopped cucumber

Peel prawns, putting shells, heads and tails into a saucepan. Reserve prawns. Cover with 940ml (1½ pints/3¾ cups) water and add lemon peel, bay leaves, mace and salt and pepper.

Bring to the boil, then cover and simmer for 30 minutes. Strain stock through a muslin-lined sieve or coffee filter paper. Return stock to rinsed-out pan. Cut squid into thin rings and chop tentacles. Add to pan and cook for 5 minutes. Set aside to cool.

Stir in spring onions, tomatoes, cucumber and reserved prawns. Season if necessary. Chill soup for at least 1 hour before serving.

Serves 4.

LEMON GRASS SOUP

175-225g (6-8oz) raw large prawns
2 teaspoons vegetable oil
625ml (20fl oz/2½ cups) light fish stock
2 thick stalks lemon grass, finely chopped
3 tablespoons lime juice
1 tablespoon fish sauce
3 kaffir lime leaves, chopped
½ fresh red chilli, seeded and thinly sliced
½ fresh green chilli, seeded and thinly sliced
½ teaspoon crushed palm sugar
coriander leaves, to garnish

Peel prawns and remove dark veins running down their backs; reserve prawns.

In a wok, heat oil, add prawn shells and fry, stirring occasionally, until they change colour. Stir in stock, bring to boil and simmer for 20 minutes. Strain stock and return to wok; discard shells. Add lemon grass, lime juice, fish sauce, lime leaves, chillies and sugar. Simmer for 2 minutes.

Add prawns and cook just below simmering point for 2-3 minutes until prawns are cooked. Serve in warmed bowls garnished with coriander.

Serves 4.

NEW ENGLAND CLAM CHOWDER

two 300g (10oz) cans clams
85g (3oz) back bacon, rinded and diced
1 onion, finely chopped
500g (1lb) potatoes, diced
300ml (10fl oz/1¼ cups) fish stock
300ml (10fl oz/1¼ cups) milk
150ml (5fl oz/⅔ cup) single (light) cream
pinch dried thyme
salt and pepper
fresh thyme leaves or paprika, to garnish

Drain clams, reserving liquid, then chop and set aside. Put bacon into a saucepan and fry over high heat until fat runs and bacon is lightly browned. Add onion and cook until soft, then add potatoes, liquid from clams, fish stock and milk. Bring to the boil, then cover and simmer for about 20 minutes, or until potatoes are tender.

Stir in cream, clams, thyme and salt and pepper, then reheat for a few minutes: do not boil. Serve garnished with thyme or paprika.

Serves 6.

WATERCRESS SOUP WITH MARIGOLDS

115g (4oz/⅔ cup) chickpeas
pinch bicarbonate of soda
3 thyme sprigs
2 tablespoons olive oil
1 leek, finely chopped
2 courgettes (zucchini), cubed
1 carrot, sliced
2 tablespoons finely chopped parsley
1¼ litres (40fl oz/4½ cups) chicken stock
115g (4oz) watercress, finely chopped
3 marigold flowers, to garnish

Put chickpeas in a bowl, cover with cold water and soak for 2 hours. Put into a large saucepan with their soaking liquid, bicarbonate of soda and thyme; add water to cover chickpeas by about 10cm (4in). Bring to boil and boil steadily for 10 minutes. Lower heat, cover pan and simmer for 30-40 minutes or until soft. Drain chickpeas and discard thyme.

In another saucepan, heat the oil. Add leek, courgettes (zucchini), carrot, parsley and chickpeas; cover and cook over gentle heat for 10 minutes to soften vegetables. Pour on chicken stock and simmer for 15-20 minutes until tender. Add watercress. Purée soup in a blender or food processor until smooth. Serve immediately, garnished with marigold petals.

Serves 6.

MARINATED OLIVES

115g (4oz) green olives
2 thin lemon slices
2 teaspoons coriander seeds
2 cloves garlic
olive oil to cover
115g (4oz) black olives
¼ red pepper
1 small hot chilli
1 sprig thyme

Place green olives in a jar. Cut each lemon slice into quarters and add to olives. Lightly crush coriander seeds and 1 clove garlic and add to the olives. Cover with olive oil and seal jar.

Place black olives in a separate jar. Crush remaining garlic clove and cut pepper and chilli into strips, removing seeds. Add to olives with sprig of thyme. Cover with olive oil and seal jar.

Leave in marinade for at least 2 days before transferring to a serving bowl and serving with other mezes. Consume within one week. The oil can be used for salad dressings and cooking.

Serves 6.

HERB &
FETA BALLS

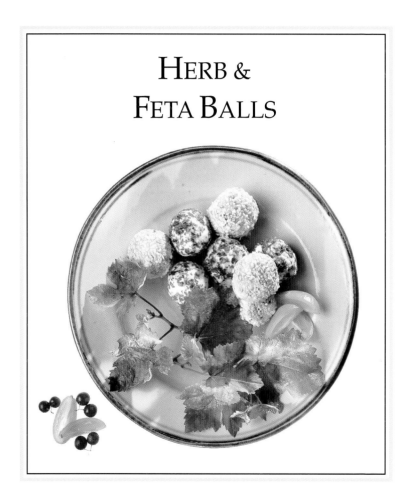

225g (8 oz) cream cheese

85g (3oz) feta cheese

1 clove garlic, crushed

1 teaspoon chopped fresh parsley

1 teaspoon chopped fresh mint

2 tablespoons sesame seeds

3 teaspoons finely chopped
fresh parsley

3 teaspoons finely chopped
fresh mint

vine leaves, to serve

In a bowl, mix together cream cheese and feta cheese until smooth. Stir in garlic, parsley and mint. Roll cheese into 20 balls. Chill for at least 1 hour. meanwhile, toast sesame seeds for garnish. Put in a frying pan and heat until seeds are golden brown, stirring frequently. Leave to cool.

To serve, mix together chopped parsley and chopped mint for garnish. Roll half cheese balls in herbs and half in toasted sesame seeds. Serve on vine leaves.

Makes 20.

CHEESE STRAWS

115g (4oz/1 cup) plain flour
pinch salt
½ teaspoon curry powder
55g (2oz/¼ cup) butter
55g (2oz/½ cup) grated Cheddar cheese
1 egg, beaten
poppy and cumin seeds, to finish

Sift flour, salt and curry powder into a bowl. Rub in butter until mixture resembles fine breadcrumbs. Add cheese and half the egg and mix to form a dough. Cover and chill for 30 minutes.

Preheat oven to 200C (400F/Gas 6). Butter several baking sheets. Roll out dough on a floured surface to 0.5cm (¼in) thickness. Cut into 7.5 × 1cm (3 × ½in) strips. Twist and place on baking sheets.

Brush straws with remaining egg. Sprinkle half the straws with poppy seeds and half with cumin seeds. Bake in the oven for 10-15 minutes until golden.

Makes 24-30.

POTTED PRAWNS

350g (12oz) peeled small prawns
salt
cayenne pepper, to taste
1 teaspoon lemon juice
½ teaspoon ground ginger
175g (6oz/¾ cup) butter
3 teaspoons finely chopped fresh chives
chives and lemon slices (optional), to garnish
French bread or buttered toast, to serve

If using thawed frozen prawns, pat dry with absorbent kitchen paper. Put prawns in a bowl with salt, cayenne pepper, lemon juice and ground ginger. Set aside in a cool place.

In a saucepan, melt butter over a very low heat. Pour the clear liquid into a bowl, leaving the milky residue in the pan. Stir in chopped chives. Leave to stand for 20 minutes.

Divide prawns between 6 small ramekin dishes. Spoon chive butter over, pressing prawns down until covered with butter. Chill until firm. Garnish with chives and lemon slices, if wished, and serve with French bread or toast.

Serves 6.

SMOKED SALMON PARCELS

225g (8oz) smoked salmon
175g (6oz) cream cheese
2 tablespoons olive oil
2 teaspoons lime juice
3 tablespoons finely chopped dill
black pepper, to taste
4 teaspoons horseradish cream
lime slices and dill sprigs, to garnish

Slightly oil four 100ml (3½fl oz/ ⅓ cup) ramekin dishes. Line each with smoked salmon, moulding it to fit dish and leaving a little extra to fold over top of dish.

Blend cream cheese with oil and lime juice. Add chopped dill, black pepper and any extra smoked salmon, chopped. Spoon in horseradish but do not mix in thoroughly; it should be distributed in hot ribbons throughout cream cheese mixture.

Place 4-5 teaspoons cream cheese mixture in each ramekin, then fold smoked salmon over top to make a neat parcel. Chill for 3-4 hours.

To serve, turn out onto a plate. Garnish with lime slices and dill.

Serves 4.

CHICKEN &
HAM MOUSSE

175g (6oz) cooked chicken, finely minced

115g (4oz) cooked ham, finely minced

1 tablespoon lemon juice

1 tablespoon chopped fresh parsley

1 tablespoon chopped fresh chives

150ml (5fl oz/⅔ cup) mayonnaise

2 teaspoons powdered gelatine

3 tablespoons chicken stock

150ml (5fl oz/⅔ cup) double (thick) cream

In a bowl, mix the chicken with the ham, lemon juice, chopped herbs and mayonnaise.

In a small pan, sprinkle the gelatine over the chicken stock and leave for 5 minutes to soften. Melt very gently over a low heat until gelatine dissolves, then cool and fold into the ham and chicken mixture.

Lightly beat the cream to form soft peaks and then carefully fold into the chicken and ham mixture. Pour the mixture into a 1 litre (35fl oz/4½ cup) mould and leave to set in the refrigerator for 2-3 hours. Unmould carefully and garnish with fresh herbs. Serve with hot crusty rolls.

Serves 4.

PRAWNS WITH GARLIC

2 tablespoons vegetable oil
5 cloves garlic, chopped
0.5cm (¼in) slice fresh root ginger, very finely chopped
14-16 large prawns, peeled, tails left on
2 teaspoons fish sauce
2 tablespoons chopped coriander leaves
freshly ground black pepper
lettuce leaves, lime juice and diced cucumber, to serve

In a wok, heat oil, add garlic and fry until browned. Stir in ginger, heat for 30 seconds, then add prawns and stir-fry for 2-3 minutes until beginning to turn opaque. Stir in fish sauce, coriander, 1-2 tablespoons water and plenty of black pepper. Allow to bubble for 1-2 minutes.

Serve prawns on a bed of lettuce leaves with lime juice squeezed over and scattered with diced cucumber.

Serves 4.

HOT MUSSELS WITH CUMIN

1.5kg (3lb) mussels
2 tablespoons vegetable oil
1 large onion, finely chopped
2.5cm (1in) piece fresh root ginger, grated
6 cloves garlic, crushed
2 fresh green chillis, seeded and finely chopped
½ teaspoon turmeric
2 teaspoons ground cumin
85g (3oz/1¾ cups) shredded fresh coconut
2 tablespoons chopped fresh coriander
coriander sprigs, to garnish

Scrub mussels clean in several changes of fresh cold water and pull off beards. Discard any mussels that are cracked or do not close tightly when tapped. Set aside.

Heat oil in a large saucepan and add onion. Fry, stirring, for 5 minutes, until soft, then add ginger, garlic, chillis, turmeric and cumin. Fry 2 minutes, stirring constantly. Add mussels, coconut and 250ml (8fl oz/ 1 cup) water and bring to the boil. Cover and cook over a high heat, shaking pan frequently, for about 5 minutes until almost all shells have opened. Discard any that do not open.

Spoon mussels into a serving dish, pour over cooking liquid and sprinkle with chopped coriander. Garnish with coriander sprigs and serve at once.

Serves 4.

SMOKED FISH PLATTER

2 smoked trout fillets
2 peppered smoked mackerel fillets
3 slices bread, toasted
25g (1oz/6 teaspoons) butter
1 teaspoon lemon juice
100g (3½ oz) can smoked oysters, drained
small lettuce leaves, lemon slices and parsley or dill, to garnish
HORSERADISH SAUCE
3 tablespoons Greek strained yogurt
2 teaspoons horseradish relish
1 teaspoon lemon juice
2 teaspoons chopped fresh parsley
pepper

Skin trout and mackerel fillets and carefully cut them into small even-sized pieces. Set them aside.

Using a small fancy cutter, cut out 4 rounds from each toast. Beat butter and lemon juice together. Spread a little on the toast rounds. Place a smoked oyster on each buttered toast round.

Arrange the pieces of smoked fish and the oysters on toast on 4 plates. Garnish each plate with a few lettuce leaves, lemon slices and sprigs of parsley or dill.

Make sauce by mixing ingredients together in a bowl. Spoon into a serving dish and serve with salads.

Serves 4.

GRAVAD LAX

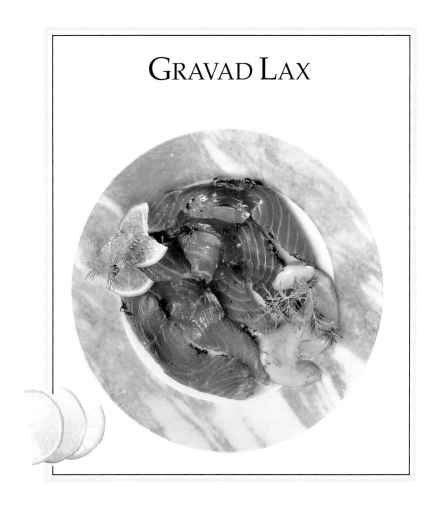

3 tablespoons sea salt
2-3 teaspoons light brown sugar
2 teaspoons crushed black peppercorns
6 tablespoons lime juice
large bunch dill
1.4-1.8kg (3-4lb) salmon, filleted, with skin
lime slices and dill sprigs, to garnish
DILL AND MUSTARD SAUCE
3 tablespoons Dijon mustard
2 tablespoons white wine vinegar
1 tablespoon sugar
150ml (5fl oz/⅔ cup) grapeseed oil
2 tablespoons finely chopped fresh dill
salt and pepper

In a small bowl, mix together salt, sugar, peppercorns and lime juice. Spread some dill in a shallow non-metallic dish and add a quarter of salt mixture. Lay one salmon fillet, skin side down, in dish. Cover with plenty of dill and spoon over half remaining salt mixture. Place remaining salmon on top, skin-side uppermost. Cover with remaining dill and pour over remaining salt mixture. Cover with greaseproof paper then plastic wrap.

Place a 900g (2lb) weight on top and leave in a cool place for 2 days, or bottom of refrigerator for 3 days, turning occasionally and spooning liquid back between fillets occasionally.

To make sauce, mix together mustard, vinegar and sugar, then gradually whisk in oil. Add chopped dill and seasoning. Drain salmon well, pat dry and trim off any hard edges. Very thinly slice salmon on bias, discarding skin. Garnish with lime slices and sprigs of dill and serve with sauce.

Serves 8.

FIVE-SPICE SALMON STEAKS

4 × 175g (6oz) salmon steaks
2 teaspoons five-spice powder
freshly ground black pepper
1 tablespoon groundnut (peanut) oil
1 clove garlic, finely chopped
2 tablespoons rice wine
1 tablespoon light soy sauce
1 teaspoon sesame oil
pared rind 1 lemon, cut into fine strips

Wash salmon steaks and pat dry with kitchen paper. Rub both sides with five-spice powder and freshly ground black pepper.

Heat oil in a non-stick or well seasoned wok, add the garlic and gently fry the salmon for 1-2 minutes on each side until salmon is lightly browned. Add the rice wine, soy sauce and sesame oil and simmer gently for 3-4 minutes until the salmon is just cooked through. Stir in lemon rind.

Remove salmon with a slotted spoon and remove and discard skin. Serve with wedges of lemon and steamed vegetables.

Serves 4.

CHICKEN BIRYANI

8 tablespoons vegetable oil
1 stick cinnamon
8 cloves
6 cardamom pods, bruised
2.5cm (1in) piece fresh root ginger, finely chopped
700g (1½lb) skinned and boned chicken, cubed
2 cloves garlic, crushed
1 teaspoon chilli powder
300ml (10fl oz/1¼ cups) natural yogurt
150ml (5fl oz/⅔ cup) chicken stock
pinch saffron strands
4 tablespoons boiling water
350g (12oz/2¼ cups) basmati rice
4 tablespoons sultanas
4 tablespoons flaked almonds
1 onion, sliced

Preheat oven to 190C (375F/Gas 5). In a flameproof casserole, heat 4 tablespoons oil and add the spices and fry for 15 seconds. Add the chicken, garlic and chilli and fry for 4 minutes. Add the yogurt, 1 tablespoon at a time, stirring between each addition until yogurt is absorbed by the spices. Add the stock and simmer for 20-25 minutes. Transfer to a bowl.

Soak the saffron in the boiling water and put to one side. Wash the rice under cold running water until the water runs clear, then cook in boiling, salted water for 3 minutes and drain.

Put 2 tablespoons oil in the casserole, spoon in a layer of rice, sprinkle with a little of the saffron water and cover with a layer of chicken. Repeat, ending with a layer of rice. Add any cooking juices left from the chicken, cover tightly and cook in the oven for 25-30 minutes.

In a pan, heat the remaining oil and fry the sultanas and almonds until golden; remove. Fry the onions until crisp and golden. Sprinkle the biryani with the almonds, onions and sultanas.

Serves 4.

41

CHICKEN & CORN FRITTERS

1 banana
1 egg
85g (3oz) cooked chicken, finely chopped
200g (7oz) can sweetcorn kernels, drained
2 spring onions, finely chopped
½ teaspoon ground cumin
2 teaspoons chopped fresh coriander
salt and cayenne pepper
85g (3oz/¾ cup) self-raising flour
oil for frying

Mash the banana. Mix in the egg, chicken, sweetcorn, spring onions, cumin, coriander, salt and a pinch of cayenne pepper. Add the flour and form a soft batter.

Heat oil in a heavy frying pan or saucepan and add spoonfuls of the mixture, cooking for about 1 minute, turning halfway through cooking, until golden brown.

Remove from the pan with a slotted spoon and drain on absorbent kitchen paper. Serve the fritters warm with a chilli dip or relish.

Serves 4.

SOUTHERN-FRIED CHICKEN

4 chicken breasts
salt and pepper
3 tablespoons paprika
2 tablespoons ground coriander
1 tablespoon ground cumin
finely grated rind and juice 1 lemon
3 tablespoons dark soy sauce
2 tablespoons chopped fresh coriander
1 teaspoon chopped fresh thyme
1 onion, finely chopped
2 cloves garlic, crushed
1 red chilli pepper, deseeded and chopped
vegetable oil for frying
85g (3oz/³⁄₄ cup) plain flour
lemon wedges and coriander sprigs, to garnish

Remove the skin from the chicken breasts. Place the chicken in a shallow dish. Make several incisions in the chicken portions and season well with salt and pepper.

In a small bowl, mix together 2 tablespoons paprika, 1 tablespoon ground coriander and 2 teaspoons ground cumin and sprinkle over the chicken. Mix the rind and juice of the lemon with the soy sauce, then add the coriander, thyme, onion, garlic and chilli. Pour over the chicken – making sure it is well covered by the mixture. Cover the dish with plastic wrap and leave to marinate for at least 3 hours or overnight.

Half fill a deep fat pan or fryer with the oil and heat to 190C (375F). Put the flour on a plate and season with salt and pepper. Add the remaining paprika, cumin and coriander and mix well. Dip the chicken pieces in the flour to thoroughly coat. Deep fry the chicken, 4 pieces at a time, for approximately 15 minutes or until chicken is golden brown and cooked through. Serve garnished with lemon wedges and coriander sprigs.

Serves 4.

GRILLED CHICKEN & HERBS

4 chicken breasts, on the bone, weighing about 175g (6oz) each
2 cloves garlic, peeled and sliced
4 fresh rosemary sprigs
6 tablespoons olive oil
grated rind and juice ½ lemon
2 tablespoons dry white wine
salt and pepper
½ teaspoon Dijon mustard
2 tablespoons balsamic vinegar
1 teaspoon sugar

Make several incisions in the chicken breasts and insert pieces of garlic and rosemary. Place the chicken breasts in a flameproof dish.

Mix together 2 tablespoons olive oil with the rind and juice of ½ lemon, the white wine and salt and pepper and pour over the chicken breasts and leave to marinate for 45 minutes. Preheat grill.

Place the chicken breast, skin-sides down, in the dish and cook under the hot grill for 5 minutes. Turn over and spoon the marinade over the top and grill for a further 10 minutes until the skin is crisp and brown. Whisk together the mustard, vinegar, sugar, salt and pepper and remaining oil. Add any cooking juices or marinade from the pan and spoon over the chicken to serve.

Serves 4.

MARINATED CHICKEN SALAD

150ml (5fl oz/⅔ cup) olive oil

4 tablespoons balsamic vinegar

2 tablespoons chopped fresh basil

2 tablespoons chopped fresh rosemary

2 cloves garlic, crushed

4 skinned and boned chicken breasts

1 red pepper (capsicum), deseeded and quartered

1 yellow pepper (capsicum), deseeded and quartered

2 courgettes (zucchini), cut into 1cm (½in) thick slices

2 large open cup mushrooms

55g (2oz/¼ cup) toasted pine nuts

8 sun-dried tomatoes

½ teaspoon sugar

salt and pepper

Mix together 4 tablespoons olive oil, 2 tablespoons vinegar, 1 tablespoon basil, 1 tablespoon rosemary and the garlic. Put the chicken into a shallow, flameproof dish and pour over the mixture. Leave for 30 minutes. Preheat grill.

Place dish of chicken under the hot grill and cook for 10-14 minutes, turning halfway through cooking until the chicken is brown and crispy; cool. Lay the peppers (capsicums), courgettes (zucchini) and mushrooms in the grill pan, brush with 2 tablespoons oil and grill for about 10 minutes, turning them once: cool.

Peel the skins from the peppers, using a sharp knife, and cut the mushrooms into quarters. Slice the chicken breasts into 2.5cm (1in) thick slices and arrange with the grilled vegetables in a dish. Sprinkle over the pine nuts and sun-dried tomatoes. In a small jug, mix the remaining herbs with the oil and vinegar. Add the sugar and season with a little salt and pepper. Pour over the chicken and marinate for 1 hour, stirring occasionally.

Serves 4.

SMOKED CHICKEN KEDGEREE

25g (1oz/6 teaspoons) butter
1 teaspoon coriander seeds, crushed
1 onion, sliced
1 teaspoon ground coriander
2 teaspoons ground cumin
85g (3oz/½ cup) long-grain rice
85g (3oz/½ cup) red lentils
550ml (20fl oz/2½ cups) chicken stock
350g (12oz) smoked chicken, coarsely chopped
juice ½ lemon
115ml (4fl oz/½ cup) natural Greek yogurt
2 tablespoons chopped fresh parsley
2 hard-boiled eggs, coarsely chopped
1 lemon, sliced, to garnish
mango chutney and poppadoms, to serve

In a large pan, melt the butter, add the crushed coriander seeds and the onion and cook over a gentle heat until slightly softened, then stir in the ground coriander, cumin, rice and lentils and coat well with the butter. Pour in the stock, bring to the boil, then cover and simmer for 10 minutes.

Remove the lid, add the chicken and continue cooking for a further 10 minutes until all the liquid has been absorbed and the rice and lentils are tender. Stir in the lemon juice, yogurt, parsley and chopped hard-boiled eggs, and heat through gently. Spoon into a warmed serving dish and garnish with lemon. Serve with mango chutney and poppadoms.

Serves 4.

MINTED MEATBALLS

1 small onion, quartered
400g (14oz) can chopped tomatoes
300ml (10fl oz/1¼ cups) chicken stock
grated rind and juice ½ large orange
2 tablespoons tomato purée (paste)
4 tablespoons chopped fresh mint
1 teaspoon sugar
1 teaspoon red wine vinegar
450 g (1 lb) raw chicken, minced
8 spring onions, finely chopped
55g (2oz/1 cup) fresh white breadcrumbs
1 small egg, beaten
2 teaspoons ground cumin
salt and pepper
oil for frying

Place the onion, tomatoes, stock, orange rind and juice, tomato purée (paste), 2 tablespoons chopped mint, sugar and vinegar, in a blender or food processor. Blend until smooth, then pour into a saucepan and simmer for 10-15 minutes.

In a large bowl, combine the chicken with the spring onions, breadcrumbs, egg, remaining 2 tablespoons chopped mint, cumin and seasonings. Using wet hands, form the chicken mixture into 40 small balls.

In a large non-stick pan, heat a little oil and fry the meatballs for about 6-8 minutes until slightly coloured all over. Remove from the pan and drain on absorbent kitchen paper. Wipe out the frying pan with absorbent kitchen paper and return the meatballs to the pan, spoon over the sauce and simmer, uncovered, for 15 minutes.

Serve on a bed of freshly cooked spaghetti, sprinkle with Parmesan cheese and garnish with mint sprigs.

Serves 4.

LAMB WITH MUSTARD & TARRAGON

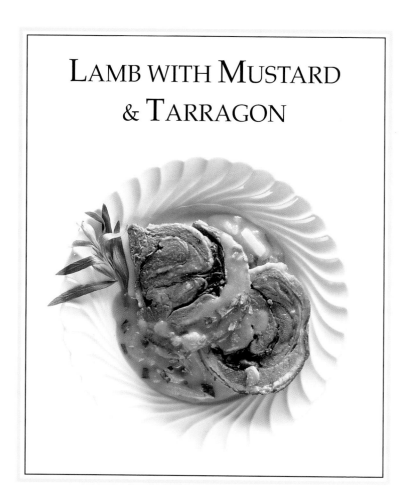

1 boned shoulder of lamb, about 2kg (4lb)
2 cloves garlic, slivered
4 teaspoons dry mustard
2 teaspoons salt
3-4 tarragon sprigs
black pepper, to taste
3 teaspoons olive oil
30g (1oz) butter
1 onion, finely sliced
200ml (7fl oz/¾ cup) white wine
3 teaspoons chopped tarragon

Preheat oven to 180C (350F/Gas 4). Make several slits in lamb and insert garlic. Mix together mustard and salt and smear half on inside of the lamb. Lay tarragon sprigs on meat and grind some black pepper over. Roll up and secure with string. Rub joint with remaining mustard and salt.

In a flameproof dish, heat oil and butter, add lamb and brown. Add onion and soften, then pour in wine; stir and scrape up all juices and sediment. Cover and cook in the oven for 2½-3 hours, to taste. Allow lamb to stand for 10 minutes before serving. Pour fat off cooking juices, then simmer for several minutes, stirring. Remove string from meat and carve; add chopped tarragon to sauce.

Serves 6-8.

ORIENTAL SPARE RIBS

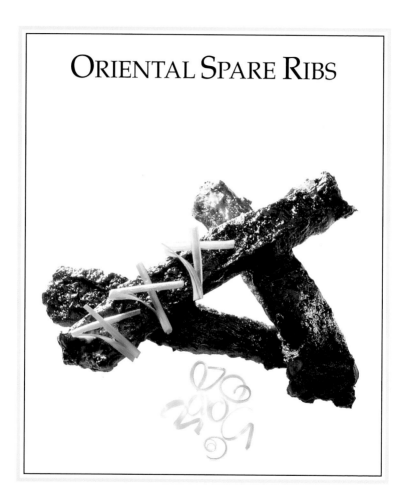

3kg (6lb) lean pork spare ribs
spring onion tassels, to garnish
SAUCE
115ml (4 fl oz/½ cup) hoisin sauce
115ml (4fl oz/½ cup) miso paste
300ml (10fl oz/1¼ cups) tomato purée (paste)
1½ teaspoons ground ginger
1½ teaspoons Chinese five-spice powder
175g (6 oz/1 cup) muscovado sugar
3 cloves garlic, crushed
1 teaspoon salt
2 tablespoons rice wine or dry sherry

Separate the ribs and trim away most of the fat.

In a bowl, combine sauce ingredients and spread all over the ribs. Put the sauced ribs in a large shallow dish. Cover with plastic wrap and leave in the refrigerator for at least 4 hours, or preferably overnight.

Place a drip pan in medium hot coals and barbecue ribs on a rack above the pan for 45-60 minutes, turning occasionally and basting with sauce. Heat any remaining sauce gently and serve separately. Garnish ribs with spring onion tassels.

Serves 8.

PORK WITH PEARS

2 tablespoons olive oil
2 onions, chopped
1kg (2.2lb) boned lean pork, cut into cubes
250ml (9fl oz/1 cup) red wine
grated rind ½ orange
½ cinnamon stick
salt and pepper
2 pears
2 teaspoons clear honey
chopped fresh coriander leaves, orange rind strips and pitta bread, to garnish

In a flameproof casserole, heat oil. Add onions; cook until soft. Push to side of pan, turn up heat and brown meat in batches. Add wine, orange rind, cinnamon stick, salt, pepper and 300ml (10fl oz/1¼ cups) water. Bring to simmering point, then cover casserole and cook for 1 hour.

Peel, core and slice pears and place on top of meat. Drizzle honey over pears. Cover pan and simmer gently for 30-40 minutes until meat is tender. Garnish with chopped coriander leaves, strips of orange rind and pieces of pitta bread.

Serves 6.

Note: This recipe is traditionally made with quinces. If quinces are available, use them instead of pears.

MINCED MEAT FINGERS

3 teaspoons pine nuts
55ml (2fl oz/¼ cup) olive oil
1 onion, finely chopped
350 g (12 oz) lean minced beef
1 teaspoon ground cinnamon
1 tablespoon chopped fresh parsley
salt and pepper
6 sheets filo pastry
Tzatziki, to serve

In a frying pan, heat pine nuts until golden. Remove from pan and set aside. Heat 2 tablespoons oil in frying pan, add onion and cook until soft. Stir in beef and cook, stirring, for a few minutes until brown all over. Add cinnamon, parsley, pine nuts, salt and pepper. Cook for a further 10 minutes, then leave to cool.

Preheat oven to 180C (350F/Gas 4). Cut each sheet of filo pastry into 3 long strips. Brush strips with remaining oil. Spread 1 teaspoon of filling in a line on one end of each strip, leaving a small margin on either side. Roll over twice and fold long sides over the edge, then continue rolling to make a tube. Place fingers on a baking sheet. Bake in the oven for 20-30 minutes until crisp and golden. Serve with Tzatziki.

Makes 18.

BEEF WITH OREGANO

2 tablespoons olive oil
115 g (4 oz) unsmoked bacon rashers, rinds removed
1 kg (2 lb) beef, cut into 10 or 12 pieces
2 onions, quartered
2 tablespoons finely chopped oregano
2 tablespoons finely chopped parsley
1 bay leaf
1 large clove garlic, crushed
115ml (4fl oz/½ cup) red wine
150g (5oz/1 cup) chopped green olives
2 tablespoons fresh breadcrumbs
grated rind 1 lemon
salt and pepper, to taste
oregano sprigs, to garnish

In a flameproof casserole large enough to take the beef in one layer, heat the oil. Add bacon and sauté until crisp; remove with a slotted spoon and set aside. Add beef and cook until evenly browned. Add onions and toss in oil for 1 minute.

Add half the oregano and parsley, the bay leaf, garlic, wine and 100ml (3½fl oz/⅓ cup) water. Cover and simmer for 2 hours. Add bacon and olives and continue cooking for 45 minutes – the stew should be fairly liquid.

Mix together breadcrumbs, lemon rind and remaining herbs and add to stew. Cook, uncovered, for a further 10-15 minutes. Season with salt and pepper. Discard bay leaf.

Garnish with oregano and serve with fresh bread and a green salad.

Serves 4.

Variation: Thyme can be added to this casserole for a stronger, more aromatic flavour. Substitute 3 teaspoons finely chopped thyme for half the oregano.

CRÈME BRÛLÉE

4 egg yolks

2½ teaspoons caster sugar

pinch cornflour

*625ml (20fl oz/2½ cups)
whipping cream*

2 vanilla pods

caster sugar for topping

frosted flowers (optional)

In a large bowl, beat egg yolks lightly with sugar and cornflour. Put cream into a saucepan. With a sharp knife, split open vanilla pods and scrape seeds into cream. Bring almost to boiling point, then pour onto yolks, beating all the time. Pour into top of a double boiler, or a bowl set over a pan of simmering water, and cook over medium heat until mixture thickens sufficiently to coat the back of spoon. Pour into shallow gratin dish. Leave to cool, then chill in the refrigerator overnight.

Two hours before serving, heat grill to very high. Cover surface of pudding thickly and evenly with sugar and place under grill until the sugar has caramelized. Chill for 2 hours. Decorate with frosted flowers, if desired.

Serves 4-6.

FLAMING FRUIT SALAD

550g (1lb/7½ cups) mixed dried fruit, such as prunes, apricots, figs, apples, pears and peaches

2 tablespoons sherry

juice ½ lemon

2 tablespoons clear honey

½ cinnamon stick

4 tablespoons brandy

85g (3oz/¾ cup) toasted almond flakes

55g (2oz/½ cup) walnuts, coarsely chopped

chilled single (light) cream or ice cream, to serve

Soak fruit overnight in 625ml (20fl oz / 2½ cups) water and the sherry.

Put fruit and soaking liquid into a saucepan with lemon juice, honey and cinnamon stick. Cover and simmer on a low heat until fruit is just tender. Discard cinnamon stick, transfer fruit to serving dish and keep warm.

In a small pan, heat brandy and set alight. While still flaming, pour it over the fruit. Scatter with almonds and walnuts and serve immediately, with cream or ice cream.

Serves 5-6.

Note: The effect of flaming brandy is to burn off the alcohol and so concentrate the flavour. It is important to warm brandy first or it will not set alight.

LAVENDER & HONEY ICE CREAM

5 lavender flower sprigs
550ml (20fl oz/2½ cups) milk
175g (6oz/¾ cup) lavender honey
4 egg yolks
150ml (5fl oz/⅔ cup) double (heavy) cream
150ml (5fl oz/⅔ cup) yogurt
lavender flowers, to decorate

Turn freezer to its coldest setting. In a saucepan, heat lavender sprigs and milk to almost boiling. Remove from heat and leave to infuse for 30 minutes. Remove lavender sprigs and bring milk back to the boil.

In a small saucepan, heat honey until just melted. In a bowl, whisk egg yolks until thick and light. Gradually add melted honey. Pour boiling milk onto egg yolk mixture, beating constantly. Pour mixture into a bowl set over a pan of boiling water. Stir for about 8 minutes until custard will coat the back of the spoon. Strain into a bowl, cover and leave to cool. Stir in cream and yogurt.

Pour mixture into an 850ml (30fl oz/ 3¾ cup) freezerproof container. Put in freezer. When sides are beginning to set, beat thoroughly. Return to freezer and repeat after 30-40 minutes. When ice cream is just beginning to solidify, beat vigorously to a smooth slush. Return to freezer. Transfer from freezer to refrigerator 20 minutes before serving. Decorate with lavender flowers.

Serves 4-6.

LEMON GERANIUM
SYLLABUB

pared rind and juice 1 lemon
12 large, scented lemon geranium leaves
425g (15fl oz/1¾ cups) double (thick) cream
85g (3oz/⅓ cup) caster sugar
115ml (4fl oz/½ cup) dry white wine
55g (2oz) ratafia biscuits
small geranium leaves and lemon rind strips or slices, to garnish

Put strips of lemon rind and geranium leaves in a small saucepan and pour over 155ml (5fl oz/⅔ cup) cream. Bring to the boil very slowly, stirring all the time. Remove from heat and allow to cool completely, stirring occasionally.

In a large bowl, put sugar, lemon juice and wine and stir until the sugar has completely dissolved. Strain cooked cream and pour into wine mixture with remaining cream, stirring continuously.

Whisk with an electric whisk until syllabub stands in soft peaks (this takes about 10-15 minutes). Divide ratafia biscuits between 6 tall glasses and spoon the syllabub on top. Decorate each glass with small geranium leaves and strips of lemon rind or lemon slices and serve the syllabub at once.

Serves 6.

LEMON & CARDAMOM CAKE

3 teaspoons cardamom seeds

2 lemons

115g (4oz/1 cup) ground almonds

55g (2oz/½ cup) dried breadcrumbs

85g (3oz/⅓ cup) caster sugar

4 eggs, separated

pinch of salt

whipping cream and shredded lemon rind, to serve

Preheat oven to 190C (375F/Gas 5). Butter a 16.5cm (6½in) round loose-bottomed cake tin.

Grind cardamom seeds in a mortar. Grate lemon rind and squeeze juice from lemons.

In a bowl, mix together ground almonds, 2 teaspoons of the ground cardamom, breadcrumbs, lemon rind and juice. Mix in the sugar. Beat egg yolks and add to almond mixture. Whisk egg whites with salt until stiff; carefully fold into the mixture. Pour into prepared tin. Bake in the oven for about 40 minutes or until a skewer inserted into the centre of the cake comes out clean. Leave to cool in tin. Serve topped with piped whipped cream and shredded lemon rind as a dessert, or plain with coffee.

Serves 6.

HONEY SPICE CAKE

150g (5oz/⅔ cup) butter or margarine

115g (4oz/¾ cup) soft light brown sugar

175g (6oz/½ cup) clear honey

200g (7oz/1¾ cups) self-raising flour

1½ teaspoons ground mixed spice

2 eggs, beaten

350g (12oz/2¼ cups) icing sugar

Preheat oven to 180C (350F/Gas 4). Grease an 850ml (30fl oz/3¾ cup) fluted ring mould. Put butter or margarine, sugar, honey and 3 teaspoons water into a saucepan. Heat gently until butter has melted and sugar has dissolved. Remove from heat and cool for 10 minutes.

Sift flour and mixed spice into a bowl. Pour in melted mixture and eggs; beat well until smooth. Pour batter into prepared tin. Bake in the oven for 40-50 minutes until well risen and a skewer inserted into the centre comes out clean. Leave to cool in the tin for 2-3 minutes, then remove to a wire rack to cool completely.

To make icing, sift icing sugar into a bowl. Stir in about 9 teaspoons water to make a smooth, flowing icing. Spoon carefully over cake so that it is evenly covered in icing.

Makes 8-10 slices.

GINGER CAKE

225g (8oz/2 cups) self-raising flour

3 teaspoons ground ginger

1 teaspoon ground cinnamon

½ teaspoon bicarbonate of soda

115g (4oz/½ cup) butter or margarine

115g (4oz/¾ cup) light soft brown sugar

2 eggs

5 teaspoons golden syrup

5 teaspoons milk

TOPPING

3 pieces stem ginger

115g (4oz/¾ cup) icing sugar

4 teaspoons stem ginger syrup

Preheat oven to 160C (325F/Gas 3). Grease a shallow oblong tin measuring 27.5 × 17.5cm (11 × 7in) and line with non-stick paper. Sift flour, ginger, cinnamon and bicarbonate of soda into a bowl. Rub in butter, then stir in sugar.

In a bowl, whisk together eggs, syrup and milk. Pour into dry ingredients and beat until smooth and glossy. Pour into prepared tin. Bake in the oven for 45-50 minutes until well risen and firm to the touch. Leave in tin for 30 minutes, then remove to a wire rack to cool completely.

Cut each piece of stem ginger into quarters and arrange on top of cake. In a bowl, mix together sifted icing sugar, ginger syrup and sufficient water to make a smooth icing. Put icing into a greaseproof paper icing bag and drizzle over top of cake. Leave to set. Cut cake into squares.

Makes 12 squares.

CARAWAY KUGELHOPF

225g (8oz/2 cups) plain flour
55g (2oz/¼ cup) caster sugar
2 teaspoons easy blend yeast
2 tablespoons caraway seeds
55ml (2fl oz/¼ cup) tepid water
115g (4oz/½ cup) unsalted butter, melted
3 eggs, beaten
icing sugar, to finish

Grease a 20cm (8in) kugelhopf mould. Sift flour into a bowl. Stir in sugar, yeast and caraway seeds. Make a well in the centre; stir in water, butter and eggs. Beat vigorously until smooth. Cover bowl with plastic wrap and leave in a warm place until doubled in size. Stir mixture and turn into prepared mould. Cover with plastic wrap and leave to rise again until doubled in size.

Preheat oven to 200C (400F/Gas 6). Remove plastic wrap. Bake kugelhopf in the oven for 20 minutes. Lower the temperature to 190C (375F/Gas 5) and bake for a further 10 minutes until well risen and golden brown. Leave in the tin for 10 minutes, then remove to a wire rack. Dust lightly with icing sugar. Serve with butter while still slightly warm.

Makes 8-10 slices.

GINGER BRANDY SNAPS

55g (2oz/¼ cup) unsalted butter

55g (2oz/¼ cup) demerara sugar

55g (2oz/2 tablespoons) golden syrup

55g (2oz/¼ cup) plain flour

½ teaspoon ground ginger

1 teaspoon brandy

FILLING

300ml (10fl oz/¼ cups) double (thick) cream

3 teaspoons stem ginger syrup

6 pieces stem ginger

Preheat oven to 180C (350F/Gas 4). Grease several baking sheets. Butter the handles of 3 or 4 wooden spoons. Put butter, demerara sugar and syrup in a saucepan and heat gently until butter has melted and sugar dissolved. Cool slightly. Sift flour and ginger into melted ingredients and stir in with the brandy. Drop teaspoonfuls of mixture, well spaced out, onto prepared baking sheets. Bake in the oven for 7-10 minutes until brandy snaps are golden.

Quickly remove brandy snaps from baking sheets and roll round spoon handles, leaving them in place until set. Slide off spoons; leave on wire racks until completely cold.

In a bowl, whisk cream with ginger syrup until thick. Put cream into a piping bag fitted with a small star nozzle. Pipe into each end of brandy snaps. Slice pieces of stem ginger and use to decorate brandy snaps.

Makes about 18.

SUGAR &
SPICE BISCUITS

225g (8oz/2 cups) plain flour
pinch of salt
½ teaspoon ground cinnamon
¼ teaspoon ground allspice
¼ teaspoon ground mace
¼ teaspoon ground cloves
½ teaspoon baking powder
115g (4oz/½ cup) caster sugar
115g (4oz/½ cup) butter
1 egg, beaten
GLAZE
1 small egg, beaten
3 teaspoons milk
2 teaspoons caster sugar
2 tablespoons granulated sugar

Butter several baking sheets. Sift flour, salt, spices, baking powder and sugar into a bowl. Rub in butter until mixture resembles fine breadcrumbs. Stir in egg; mix by hand to form a soft dough.

Roll out dough on a floured surface to 0.3cm (⅛in) thick. Using fancy biscuit cutters, cut out as many shapes as possible from dough. Place on baking sheets. Re-knead and re-roll trimmings; cut out more shapes to make 32 in total. Refrigerate shapes for 30 minutes. Preheat oven to 180C (350F/Gas 4).

To make glaze, stir together egg, milk and caster sugar in a small bowl. Brush glaze over each biscuit, then sprinkle with half the granulated sugar. Bake in the oven for 15-20 minutes until lightly browned. Remove from oven and immediately sprinkle with remaining granulated sugar. Using a palette knife, carefully remove biscuits from sheets to wire racks to cool.

Makes 32.

DOSA

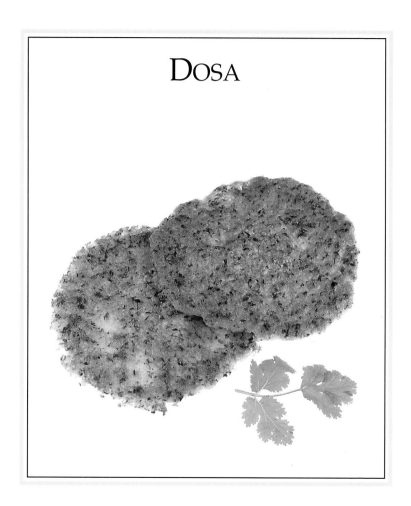

55g (2oz/⅓ cup) urad dhal (mung beans, split not husked)
150g (5oz/1 cup) long-grain rice
2 spring onions, finely chopped
2 tablespoons chopped fresh coriander
2.5cm (1in) piece fresh root ginger, grated
1 fresh green chilli, seeded and chopped
½ teaspoon salt
about 3 tablespoons vegetable oil
coriander leaves, to garnish

Wash dhal and rice thoroughly and put into separate bowls. Add 500ml (16fl oz/2 cups) water to each and leave to soak for 3 hours. Drain well.

Put dhal in a blender or food processor fitted with a metal blade. Add 90ml (3fl oz/⅓ cup) water and process until smooth. Purée rice with 90ml (3fl oz/⅓ cup) water in same way. Mix purées together in a large bowl, cover with a damp cloth and set aside at room temperature for about 12 hours.

Stir in onions, coriander, ginger, chilli, salt and about 3 tablespoons water to make a batter. Heat a 15cm (6in) frying pan, brush with a little oil, then spoon in 2-3 tablespoons batter and spread into a 10cm (4in) circle. Cook over a high heat for about 3 minutes, turning over with a fish slice after half the time, until browned. Cover with a dry cloth while cooking remainder. Serve warm, garnished with coriander leaves.

Makes about 12.

CHEESE BUNS

800g (1¾lb/7 cups) strong white bread flour

1 sachet easy blend dried yeast

2 teaspoons salt

2 teaspoons caster sugar

2 tablespoons olive oil

sesame seeds, to decorate

CHEESE FILLING

350g (12oz) kefalotiri cheese, grated

115g (4oz) haloumi cheese, finely grated

3 teaspoons plain flour

1 teaspoon baking powder

1 tablespoon chopped fresh mint

¼ teaspoon freshly grated nutmeg

4 eggs, beaten

To make the filling, place cheeses in a bowl. Add flour, baking powder, mint and nutmeg to cheese. Stir in most of beaten egg to make a stiff paste.

To make the dough, sift flour into a bowl. Stir in yeast, salt and sugar. Add oil and 425ml (15fl oz/scant 2 cups) tepid water. Mix together, then turn dough onto a floured surface and knead for 10 minutes until smooth and elastic. Divide into 16 pieces; roll out each piece to a 10cm (4in) circle.

Place a little filling in centre of each circle. Pull dough up on 3 sides to make a tricorn shape, with filling showing in centre. Pinch corners together well. Place on oiled baking sheets, cover with oiled plastic wrap and leave in a warm place until doubled in size.

Preheat oven to 230C (450F/Gas 8). Brush buns with remaining beaten egg. Scatter with sesame seeds. Bake for 12-15 minutes until golden brown.

Makes 16.

FRESH MANGO CHUTNEY

2 mangoes
1 red chilli, seeded and finely sliced
25g (1oz/¼ cup) cashew nuts, chopped
25g (1oz/¼ cup) raisins
2 tablespoons chopped fresh mint
pinch asafoetida
½ teaspoon ground cumin
¼ teaspoon cayenne pepper
½ teaspoon ground coriander
mint sprigs, to garnish

Peel and stone mangoes, then very thinly slice flesh. Put mango slices in a bowl with chilli, cashew nuts, raisins and mint and stir gently. In a small bowl, mix asafoetida, cumin, cayenne and coriander together, then sprinkle over mango mixture.

Stir gently to coat mango mixture in spices, then cover and chill for 2 hours. Serve chilled, garnished with mint sprigs.

Makes about 250g (8oz).

HOT BUTTERED RUM

4 cinnamon sticks

4 teaspoons light soft brown sugar

115ml (4fl oz/½ cup) dark rum

625ml (20fl oz/2/½ cups) cider

25g (1oz/6 teaspoons) butter

1 teaspoon ground mace

4 lemon slices

Divide cinnamon sticks, sugar and rum between 4 warm, heatproof glasses or mugs.

Place cider in a saucepan and heat until very hot, but not boiling. Fill each glass or mug almost to the top with cider.

Add a knob of butter, a sprinkling of mace and a lemon slice to each glass or mug. Stir well and serve hot.

Serves 4.

APPLE & ALE MULL

1kg (2lb) cooking apples

1.25 litres (40fl oz/5 cups) ginger
ale or ginger beer

6 whole cloves

1 blade mace

1 teaspoon grated nutmeg

½ teaspoon ground ginger

3 strips orange peel

red and green apple slices and
lemon slices, to decorate

Preheat oven to 200C (400F/Gas 6). Wash apples and remove stalks. Arrange on a baking sheet and cook in the oven for 30-40 minutes until soft. Place apples in a saucepan and mash them. Add ginger ale or ginger beer, cloves, mace, nutmeg, ginger and orange peel. Bring to boil, remove from heat and leave until cool. Strain apple mixture through a nylon sieve into a bowl, pressing through as much apple as possible.

Just before serving, return apple and ale mixture to a clean saucepan and heat until hot enough to drink. Float red and green apple slices and lemon slices on top and serve in heat-proof glasses or mugs.

Serves 8.

BOURBON MINT JULEP

2 msrs. bourbon
5 mint sprigs
4 teaspoons sugar
ice cubes
1 dash dark rum or brandy
slice lemon

Mix bourbon, 4 sprigs of mint and sugar in small glass. Pour into glass filled with ice cubes and stir until outside of glass becomes frosted. Top with dash of dark rum or brandy. Garnish with remaining sprig of mint and slice of lemon. Serve with straws.

Makes 1.

INDEX